Dear Parent:
Your child's love of reading starts here!

Every child learns to read in a different way and at his or her own speed. Some go back and forth between reading levels and read favorite books again and again. Others read through each level in order. You can help your young reader improve and become more confident by encouraging his or her own interests and abilities. From books your child reads with you to the first books he or she reads alone, there are I Can Read Books for every stage of reading:

SHARED READING
Basic language, word repetition, and whimsical illustrations, ideal for sharing with your emergent reader

BEGINNING READING
Short sentences, familiar words, and simple concepts for children eager to read on their own

READING WITH HELP
Engaging stories, longer sentences, and language play for developing readers

READING ALONE
Complex plots, challenging vocabulary, and high-interest topics for the independent reader

I Can Read Books have introduced children to the joy of reading since 1957. Featuring award-winning authors and illustrators and a fabulous cast of beloved characters, I Can Read Books set the standard for beginning readers.

A lifetime of discovery begins with the magical words "I Can Read!"

Visit www.icanread.com for information
on enriching your child's reading experience.

To Sarah, Sam, and Eli, with much love
—K.K.

For my Dad, Robert Carter
—A.C.

I Can Read® and I Can Read Book® are trademarks of HarperCollins Publishers.

The Best Seat in First Grade
Text copyright © 2020 by Katharine Kenah
Illustrations copyright © 2020 by Abby Carter

Library of Congress Control Number: 2019950277
ISBN 978-0-06-268645-9 (trade bdg.)—ISBN 978-0-06-268644-2 (pbk.)

Book design by Honee Jang
          20 21 22 23 24 LSC 10 9 8 7 6 5 4 3 2 1   ❖   First Edition

I Can Read!

BEGINNING 1 READING

The
BEST SEAT
in First Grade

by Katharine Kenah
pictures by Abby Carter

HARPER

An Imprint of HarperCollins*Publishers*

Sam was too excited to sit still.

He nearly fell off his chair.

It was the first day of first grade,
and he had news to share!

"I lost two teeth," said Ollie.

"It was my birthday," said Sophie.

"I got new glasses," said Miguel.

"I read six books," said Nina.

"I went to soccer camp," said Lily.

Sam said, "Our elephant had a baby.

Her name is Daisy."

"Wow!" said their teacher, Mr. Leon.

"No way!" said Ollie and Sophie.

"No one has an elephant," said Nina.

Lily and Miguel stared at Sam.

"Daisy is REAL!" shouted Sam.

Mr. Leon's class worked hard.

In science everyone drew habitats.

Sam drew an elephant habitat.

It had a lake and lots of grass.

"Daisy can swim," said Sam.

"How do you know?" asked Nina.

In language arts they wrote poems.

Sam wrote one about elephants.

"Elephants use their trunks to play

and eat and hold things every day."

"How do you know?" asked Ollie.

"I watch Daisy!" said Sam.

During math everyone worked
with weights and rulers.

"A grown male giraffe can be
eighteen feet tall," said Nina.

Sam said, "When Daisy is grown,
she'll weigh more than a car!"

One Friday Mr. Leon said,

"Next week is our trip to the zoo.

Pick an animal to make out of clay.

When we get back,

we'll make our own zoo."

Everyone shouted, "YAY!"

Sam couldn't wait to go to the zoo.

He had a surprise for his class!

Finally, it was zoo day.
When they got to the zoo,
the first graders entered
the Hidden Jungle.

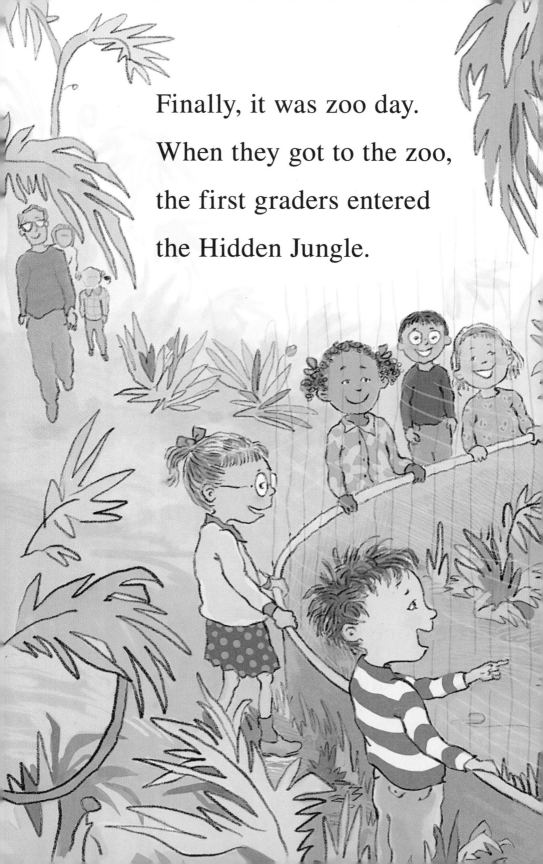

Everyone laughed at the monkeys climbing and jumping.

It looked like a monkey circus.

"Come on," said Sam.

"There's Frozen World."

Everyone went to the Antarctica exhibit

and waddled like the penguins.

The rain forest was next.

It was warm, leafy,

and filled with tropical birds.

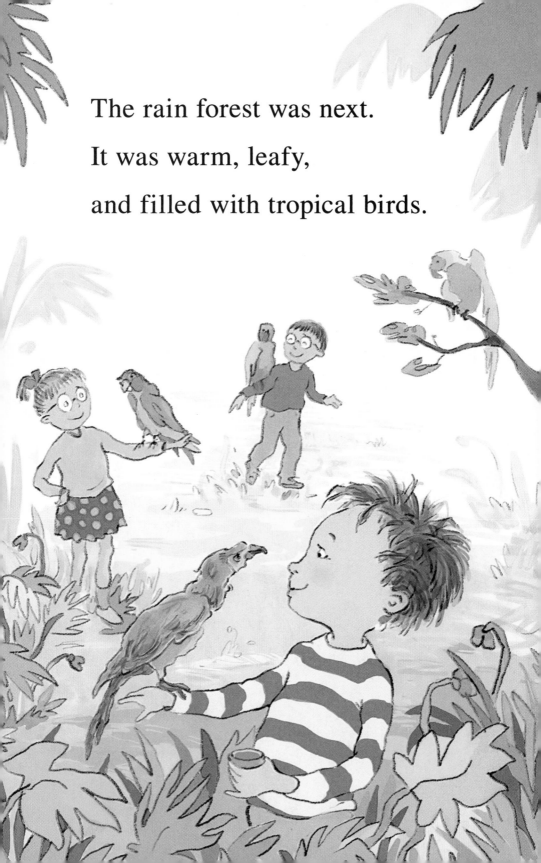

"Awesome Africa is next," said Sam. The first graders watched lion cubs playing near their mother.

They saw giraffes pulling leaves
off the branches of tall trees
and said "Hello!" to the hippo.

Finally, Sam said, "We're here."

"Where?" asked his class.

They looked up and saw elephants!

The elephants were eating grass
and moving softly together.
They were wrinkled, gray,
and magnificent.

Their zookeeper waved at Sam.

She was spraying the elephants

with a hose.

"They like showers," said Sam.

"How do you know?" asked Sophie.

"That's my mom," said Sam.

"She takes care of the elephants."

A little elephant was nearby,
pushing a ball into puddles.
"Hi, Daisy!" yelled Sam.
Sam's class shouted, "Daisy is real!"
He smiled and said, "I know."

Daisy stopped and sniffed the air.

"She knows Sam's here," said Nina.

As soon as they got back to school,
the first graders made their zoo.
It had a clay lion, hippo, monkey,
penguin, and giraffe.

It also had six baby elephants.

They were all named Daisy.

For the rest of the year Sam sat
between his friends and the zoo.
He had the best seat in first grade.